WHAT DOES
good
LOOK LIKE?

DR PAIGE WILLIAMS

Copyright © 2025 Dr Paige Williams
The moral rights of the author have been asserted.

All rights reserved. This book may not be reproduced in whole or in part, stored, posted on the internet or transmitted in any form or by any means, electronic, mechanical, photocopying, recording or other, without written permission from the author.

Please note, you should use this information as you see fit, and at your own risk. The author has taken every reasonable precaution to verify the material in this book and assumes no liability for the content herein to the extent legally permissable.

 A catalogue record for this book is available from the National Library of Australia

First published in 2024 by Dr Paige Williams, Torquay, Australia
Design and typesetting by Wholehearted Marketing

For more information about this title, contact:

Dr Paige Williams
paige@drpaige.au
www.drpaige.au

ISBN 978-0-6486419-0-2 (paperback)
ISBN 978-0-6486419-1-9 (ebook)

"Do you know where you're going to?
Do you like the things that
life is showing you?
Where are you going to?
Do you know?

Do you get what you're hoping for?
When you look behind you,
there's no open doors
What are you hoping for?
Do you know?"

Theme From Mahogany
(Do You Know Where You're Going To?)

This book is an invitation.

An invitation to reflect, to question, and to explore what 'good' looks like—for you, for your relationships, for your leadership, and for your world.

There's no single right way to engage with this book, and certainly no need to read it in order. Instead, let curiosity guide you. Open to a page that draws your attention. Start with a question that speaks to where you are right now. Follow the thread of insight and reflection as it unfolds for you.

The contents list offers a series of questions—each one a doorway into a different aspect of what 'good' might look like in different contexts. Some questions may challenge you. Others may affirm what you already know deep inside. And some may open up entirely new ways of thinking about yourself and the world around you.

This book isn't about giving you the answers. It's about helping you uncover the questions that matter most.

Use it as a catalyst for reflection, contemplation, and writing. Let it prompt journal entries, spark deep conversations, or simply sit with you in quiet moments of thought.

There is no rush. No final destination to reach. What 'good' looks like is always evolving—shaped by our experiences, our learning, and the way we choose to show up.

So take your time. Start where you feel drawn. Trust that the questions you engage with will lead you to insights that matter. And most importantly—enjoy the journey.

CONTENTS

Good Question!	2
Rules for Good	6
Too much of a Good thing	10
Good Expectations	16
Good with others	20
Good Enough	24
Not Good Enough	28
Silence: Not Good	34
Good Choosing	38
Good Chewing	42
Good Signals	48
A Good View	52
Good Bad	56
In Good Conscience	60
The Good Space	66
Good News	70
Good Job!	76
Ignorance is ~~Bliss~~ Good…?	80
Good Stories	84
Hoping for Good	88

good
QUESTION!

Every action is preceded by a question. Just think about your morning... *Set an alarm or not...? Hit snooze or get up? Toast or cereal for breakfast?*

Many of these questions are unconscious, but because we have a natural negativity bias *What's wrong? What's missing? And what needs fixing?* is often what's being asked. And while these deficit-focused questions may help identify the problems we're facing, they rarely generate the energy, commitment and momentum we need to make progress.

Which is why finding answers is not enough.

We need to bring awareness to the questions we're asking.

Being mindful of our questions allows us to choose ones that invite us to see the good, the true and the possible; questions that help us uncover our strengths, get clear about our hopes, and find the willingness and motivation to take ownership of the changes we want to create.

Asking and answering what 'good' looks like invites us to understand where we find joy, love, meaning and purpose. Our sense of community and belonging, our personal relationships and goals. How well we know ourselves and how we want to connect with others.

Are you ready to explore what good looks like for you?

What does good look like for you right now?
Where do you find joy, love, meaning
and purpose?

WHAT DOES GOOD LOOK LIKE?

RULES FOR
good

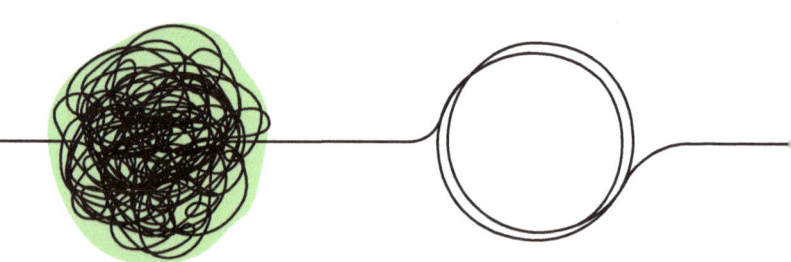

Life is complex. It's understandable to feel overwhelmed at times.

In my book *"Becoming Antifragile,"* I advocate for 'life rules' or heuristics to help us untangle complexity and make decisions, even when the consequences are unclear.

What do life rules look like?

I have one around Assuming Positive Intent. It's based on my belief that people are inherently good, and are doing the best they can with what they have available in this moment – whether that's time, energy, attention or emotional regulation.

Choosing this orientation saves me the emotional energy of trying to second guess their agenda, and cuts through potential drama. It's an invitation for them to be the person that I'm (positively) assuming they are, and step into a space of 'universal love'.

Am I ever wrong? For sure. But far less than you might think.

I have other life heuristics to help me live my core values of Truth, Honour and Love, and I draw on them every day. The benefit of life rules is that when I'm tired or frustrated, they create clarity and space for me to see other perspectives and make good choices about what comes next and how I choose to show up.

What 'life rules' could help you create clarity and space to show up as the best version of you – even when it's hard?

WHAT DOES GOOD LOOK LIKE?

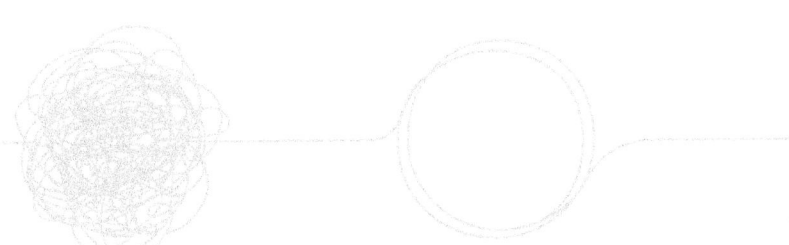

TOO MUCH OF A good THING

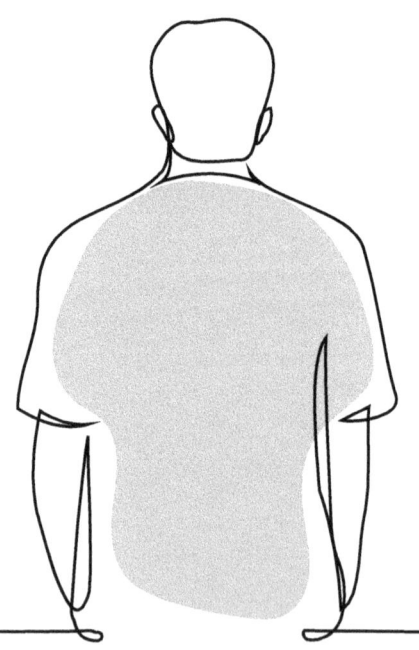

Even once we know 'what good looks like', why don't we do it?

The uncomfortable truth is that we turn away from 'good' when it becomes too hard... too much... or perhaps too wonderful. And in turning away, we limit potential, progress and performance. We place a ceiling on possibility and joy.

None of which makes sense.

Without challenges and volatility, we become weaker. *We make ourselves fragile when we always overprotect and avoid stress and challenge.*

We often learn more from our mistakes and failures than from our successes. *When we avoid small mistakes, it makes the impact and fallout of the big ones more severe.*

We also need to include *experiencing*, *expressing*, and intentionally *encouraging joy-filled moments* part of our 'best ever' life and leading development plans.

Experiences that create joy, awe and love influence our experience and outcomes at every level of our lives both personally and professionally. From creativity and energy, resilience and relationships to self-confidence and self-regulation.

It's not just about the intensity of emotions; it's also about the frequency. We need to intentionally seek, notice and prioritise opportunities for small 'jolts of joy' every day.

What 'jolts of joy' can you seek out to bring more 'good' into your life?

WHAT DOES GOOD LOOK LIKE?

"For me, forgiveness and compassion are always linked: how do we hold people accountable for wrongdoing and yet at the same time remain in touch with their humanity enough to believe in their capacity to be transformed?"

bell hooks

good
EXPECTATIONS

"We need to let go of the idea that we can change large complex systems" is one of the uncomfortable truths I often share as I work with leaders.

Railing against systems that are unfit, unfair and under-resourced is a never-ending task. The time, energy and attention that we pour into it limits our performance and potential, and leaves us depleted in our relationships – with ourselves, with others and with life.

Leadership and Systems researcher and author Meg Wheatley, suggests that rather than focusing on trying to change and transform large, complex systems, leaders can instead focus on creating 'islands of sanity' within our sphere of influence.

Yes, there may be gaps between our expectations of how things 'should' be and the reality of how they are.

However, orienting ourselves and our teams toward possibility and progress that we can directly influence, generates confidence, energy and momentum.

Where could you create an island of sanity to lead yourself and others toward possibility and progress?

WHAT DOES GOOD LOOK LIKE?

good
WITH OTHERS

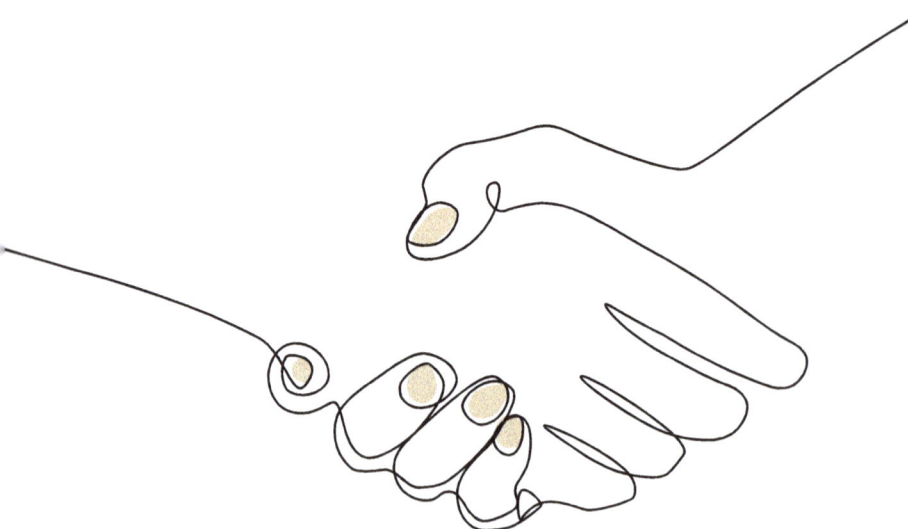

Truth be told, I'm not one for collaboration.

Past experiences with poor communication, mismatched workloads, and a lack of ownership have left a lasting stain on my perspective.

And yet I know that we are better together – we are better through collaboration.

Collaboration invites us to acknowledge that we don't have all the answers. That we have a better chance of success if, rather than taking control to facilitate a move to action, we work from a space of 'not knowing' whilst intentionally seeking the experience, knowledge and wisdom of others.

I've found holding these three questions helps me have the right orientation towards collaboration and creates it with others too:

1. What is the most valuable contribution I can make at this time?
2. Are the expectations of myself and others clear, clean, and realistic?
3. How can I be deeply committed and completely unattached in this process?

The uncomfortable truth that I've come to accept is that whilst collaborating may at times feel like it slows me down, I know that the result is better – for me and the outcomes we want to achieve, together.

What does good collaboration look like for you?
How are you a good collaborator?

WHAT DOES GOOD LOOK LIKE?

good
ENOUGH

There's a big difference between *having intentions* and *leading and living intentionally*.

We all have daily intentions – what we *plan* to do, what we *could* do. In contrast, *leading and living intentionally* requires purposeful action. The good intentions we hold in our head are meaningless without the action to bring them to life. When our positive intent is put into action in the world, then we are *leading and living intentionally*.

It can feel risky to take decisive, bold action. But make no mistake, we lead through action.

Leading is a verb.

Our role as leaders is to create order and clarity, which actually comes through action rather than preceding it.

Do they need to be big steps? No. Small can be beautiful.

Do they need to be perfect? No. Good enough is exactly that.

Do they need to be on purpose? Yes. In all its meanings – purpose-filled and intentional.

Small, perfectly imperfect actions that support positive purposeful progress.

What small 'good enough' actions can you intentionally take to make purposeful progress?

WHAT DOES GOOD LOOK LIKE?

NOT good ENOUGH

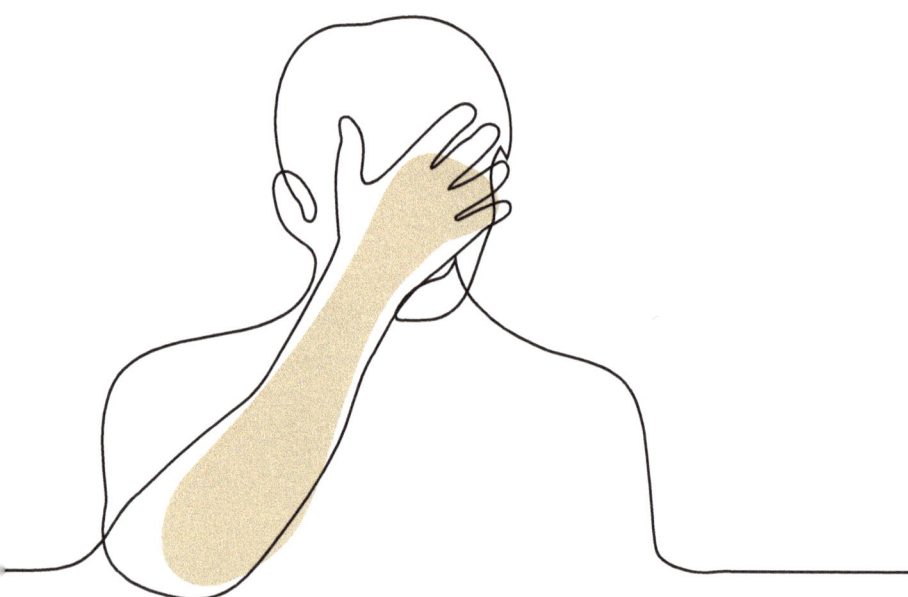

There is a word in the world that strikes me to the core... a real punch to the gut ... a wobble to my confidence and sense of identity.

It's the D-word. Disappointment.

We experience disappointment when the world doesn't show up as we believed it was going to or as we believe it should. This gap between our expectations and the reality in front of us could be called the Gap of Disappointment, but it often shows up as anger, frustration and a cycle of name, shame and blame. It makes and keeps us fragile and is a black pit for time, attention and energy.

What service could there be possibly in all of this...?

While certainly painful, disappointment may be an opportunity for self-reflection. Did we communicate expectations clearly? Were they reasonable? Realistic? Relevant?

As we become clear about what's ours to own in the disappointment and what can appropriately be asked of others – whether that be action, accountability or support – there is the possibility that we are better from our experience of disappointment... bigger... gentler... wiser.

What good has come from your experiences of disappointment?

WHAT DOES GOOD LOOK LIKE?

"The question in disappointment is whether we allow it to bring us to ground, to a firmer sense of ourselves, a surer sense of our world, and what is good and possible for us in that world, or whether we experience it only as a wound that makes us retreat from further participation."

David Whyte, *Consolations – The Solace, Nourishment and Underlying Meaning of Everyday Words.*

SILENCE = NOT good

We are wired for avoidance and have a natural aversion to mistakes, failures and the feelings of shame and embarrassment that can come with them.   There is a cost to these experiences that simply doesn't exist if we maintain silence.

So, it's not surprising that speaking up feels risky and silence feels the safer bet. Because in the moment, silence is cost free.

But there is a significant hidden cost to silence.

When people stop talking it means they're not sharing their ideas, their thoughts, their questions, their concerns, the challenges they see coming and the opportunities ahead. It means that our collective wisdom and learning are not being harnessed to help us navigate the future more effectively.

It means whilst bodies are in the room, hearts and minds are not.

And yet we know that one of the most important strategies for avoiding failures is encouraging a preference for speaking up openly and quickly about small things before they snowball into larger failures.

We cannot address what remains unspoken, unacknowledged and beneath the surface.

This silence is not golden.

Where and with whom do you experience 'ungolden' silence? How might you seek to understand what is unspoken and beneath the surface?

WHAT DOES GOOD LOOK LIKE?

good
CHOOSING

When things are going well it can be easy to act effectively, treat ourselves and others in ways that create secure relationships, and do the things that make life better in the long term rather than worse.

But as challenging situations and difficult thoughts and feelings arise, it's tempting to slip into mindsets, attitudes and behaviours that pull us off track.

How, in the complexity and day-to-day reality of work and life, can we make 'good' choices?

The Choice Points framework by Dr Russ Harris is helpful in identifying actions that move us towards the life we want to live and the person we want to be ('towards moves') and actions that move us away from that life and that person ('away moves').

We have a choice moment to moment to make towards or away moves, but of course a critical part of that is being clear about what good looks like.

It doesn't have to be perfect – good enough is sometimes exactly that.

It doesn't have to be big – doing what we can where we can is often most effective.

And it doesn't need to be completely defined – a direction to move in may be all we need.

Where can you choose to make moves 'towards' to your desired self and life?

WHAT DOES GOOD LOOK LIKE?

good
CHEWING

One of my favourite books to read to my children as they were growing up was "We're Going on a Bear Hunt" by Michael Rosen. It tells of a family, going on an adventure to find a bear and the obstacles they face as they do... squelchy mud, swirling snow and swooshy grass. As the family faces each obstacle they realise they *'Can't go over it... Can't go under it... Got to go through it.'*

It's a great metaphor for the roadblocks we get in life too.

We often try to 'go over it' by ignoring that there's an issue, or 'go under it' by squashing what we truly feel. We can even try to 'go around it' by distracting ourselves with things like food, drink and social media.

The problem is when we take any of these paths of avoidance, we miss out on the gift that is the experience of going through it.

I call this experience 'chewing'.

Chewing often involves unearthing deeply held beliefs and perspectives about the world, myself and relationships with others. It allows me to choose who I wish to be moving forward, and gives me psychological 'nutrients' that my future self will thank me for.

It reminds me that navigating my way 'through' difficulties might just be what good looks like.

Do you recognise you may be avoiding difficulties right now? What might going 'through' this difficulty ask of you? What might you need to 'chew' on?

WHAT DOES GOOD LOOK LIKE?

"A leader takes people where they want to go. A great leader takes people where they don't necessarily want to go, but ought to be."

Rosalynn Carter

good
SIGNALS

Closed minds and attachment to ideas, experiences and beliefs creates defensiveness and divide. As leaders, we have the opportunity to build bridges of perspective and understanding with and between our people.

My friend and conscious communication expert Jem Fuller explores how small steps in awareness can make big impacts in how we communicate. Here are three favourites from our conversations together:

Create Shared Understanding: Did you know that the Latin root of 'communication' is 'Communis,' meaning to make common or share? Rather than just broadcasting your position or opinion, this invites us to focus on the purpose of our communication, and create high-quality signal rather than low-quality noise.

Energetic Communication: How we show up with others creates the energetic atmosphere of what's communicated. It's more than just body language! Being present to the moment and aware of what you're feeling, thinking and experiencing is key.

Self-Care: Because of the power dynamics involved, when leaders communicate it has consequences. Regular self-care, such as pausing to breathe, creates moments of equanimity that allow us to keep doing the work of creating our energetic atmosphere. We self-care so that we can care for others and listen deeply with understanding.

How can your conversations prioritise shared understanding?
Is your energy communicating what you want and need it to?
Is it in alignment with your words?
What could you do to self-care today?

WHAT DOES GOOD LOOK LIKE?

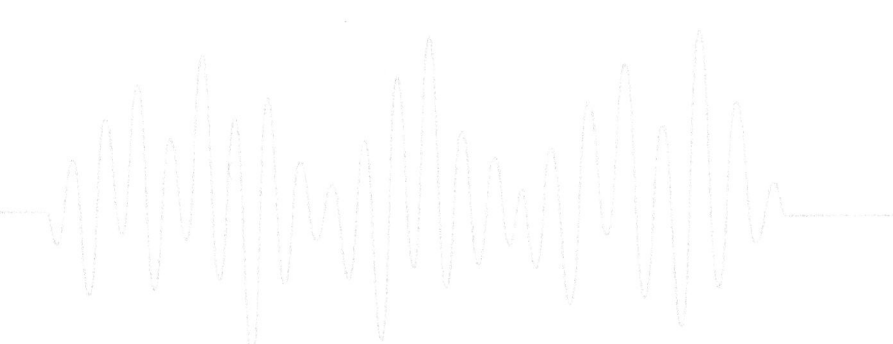

A good
VIEW

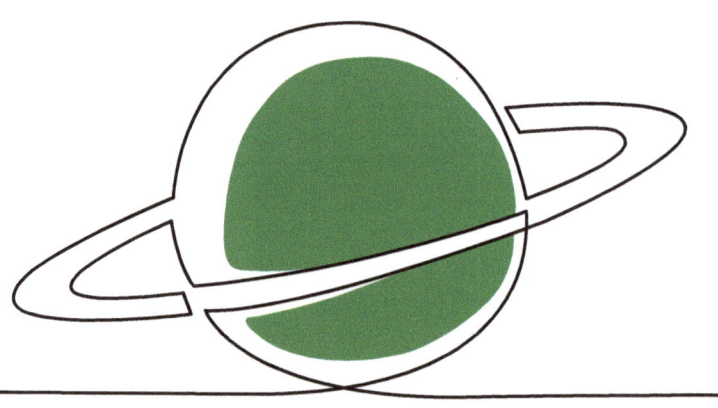

I was at a high-level online meeting of peers that I respected and admired. While it's more my style to listen, learn and only contribute when I feel I have something that really adds value, in this moment I felt I did – and so I raised my hand.

But I wasn't invited to share my contribution.

I was angry... furious. No. More than that, I was embarrassed. I felt humiliated. I felt I'd been ignored on purpose... that this was a power play and I was being deliberately excluded from the conversation. I was so triggered, I was unable to contribute further to the meeting.

My ego was standing in the way.

To be our best, we need to let go of what author Michael Singer calls the 'ego mind' that personalises everything, and interact with the reality in front of us.

We are not the centre of anyone's universe other than our own. Nobody is listening, nobody is interested, and nobody cares about what is going on for you. Because they are the centre of their universe, not you.

With this in mind, we can let go of any personal reaction – recognise the ego mind in play and stop it before it gains momentum.

We can focus on making the best contribution possible in that moment.

How does your ego prevent you from showing up in your leadership?
What practices can you use to stop it gaining momentum in these moments?

WHAT DOES GOOD LOOK LIKE?

good
BAD

You can't always get what you want... It's a reality of life, and whether we like it or not, there are often constraints in the world that we have to work with.

But rather than being an obstacle to better performance, research has found that we can actually benefit from some level of constraints; it's only when constraints become too high that they stifle creativity and innovation.

Here are three ways I've found to use constraints to my advantage:

Time and Task: Placing constraints on 'what' needs to be achieved by 'when' establishes clear expectations, while leaving the 'how' open to creativity and innovation.

Constructive Conflict: Where there are two or more seemingly conflicting outcomes that appear impossible to deliver together, use this to create a fundamental re-evaluation of the solution.

Share the Load: Fostering psychological and psychosocial safety to invite others' input allows for productive conversations about how best to navigate the constraints to your advantage.

We can't always get what we want, but maybe leveraging constraints can help us focus on getting what we need.

Where are you currently
experiencing constraints? What are they?
How could you use them to your advantage?

WHAT DOES GOOD LOOK LIKE?

IN good
CONSCIENCE

Who we are is how we show up.

In the big moments and the little ones; the moments that matter and the moments that slip by unnoticed. With colleagues and peers... Family and friends... Your nearest and dearest.

Do you recognise you... know who the true you is?

It's hard to stay anchored to who you are in the swirl of chaos and complexity. And yet it becomes even more critical as we lead ourselves and others through these moments.

MIT professors Edgar Schein and Warren Bennis have found that feeling safe inside ourselves is essential for us to feel secure in our relationships and capable of adapting how we respond to shifting contexts, situations and challenges.

This personal psychological safety frees you to be less dependent on the opinions and behaviours of others and the environments you are in. It allows you to control the only factor that is ever really within your control – yourself.

But how can we develop it?

By knowing who you are. The True You. The you that shines in your strengths and knows and loves your shadows. and perhaps developing a guiding heuristic, such as a Personal Code, to ground you to your 'true you' so that you can show up as you want to through turbulent times.

What does it look like when you
shine in your strengths?
What shadows do you know and love?
What would it mean for you to lead from
the grounded space of True You?

WHAT DOES GOOD LOOK LIKE?

"People all seek to know what they do not know yet;
they ought rather to
seek to know what they know already."

Zhuangzi

THE good SPACE

A close friend was navigating a challenging situation at work with one of their leaders, and it wasn't going well. My friend was forced to concede and be the bigger person again and again and again – for the sake of their team and any future relationship with that leader.

I was outraged on their behalf! It wasn't fair. It wasn't right. But it was their reality, and me adding to the emotional drama wasn't going to help.

And so I learned to hold space.

Author and teacher Heather Plett explains, *"When we hold space for other people, we open our hearts, offer unconditional support, and let go of judgement and control."*

For leaders this can be challenging.

We are often asked to provide solutions and problem solve. Holding space can feel like 'doing nothing'. But far from being passive, holding space is about intentionally creating a safe environment where growth and development can naturally occur. It requires total presence, absolute invisibility and letting go of any personal agenda.

So next time a friend, colleague, your partner or one of your team is struggling, rather than offering advice or solving the problem for them, just pause. Take a deep breath. Hold your tongue... and offer your presence.

With whom could you hold space and create the safety for them to struggle and grow?

WHAT DOES GOOD LOOK LIKE?

good
NEWS

Have you ever wondered how some leaders are able to 'read the landscape' – almost as if they have a crystal ball – and elegantly adjust by reinventing themselves, innovating new ideas, and meeting new market needs? They seem able to navigate struggle and challenge, whilst others get caught up spinning their wheels or collapsing under the pressure?

In my professional and personal life, I've experienced ups and downs, challenges and opportunities, joy and sadness. Some of these I handled better and survived more intact than others. Some helped me learn and grow in ways that enabled me to thrive.

Why is this?

I've come to realise that whilst I experienced struggle through many of them, for some of them I chose to suffer too.

It can be easy to assume that all struggles lead to suffering, but this isn't true.

Struggle can offer growth opportunities where we are more likely to strive, evolve and be innovative. Suffering is the inability to accept what is.

Struggle may be an inevitable part of life, however suffering is entirely optional. Because suffering is self-generated and self-perpetuating. It can also be self-correcting.

By becoming aware of your internal dialogue while facing struggle, you can choose another path.

Can you identify a recent experience of struggle? Did you accept your reality and avoid suffering? How might this work for you in future?

WHAT DOES GOOD LOOK LIKE?

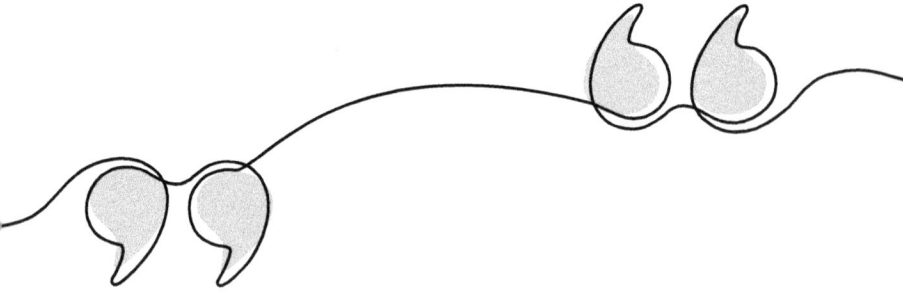

"People suffer because they are caught in their views. As soon as we release those views, we are free and we don't suffer anymore."

Thich Nhat Hanh

good
JOB!

How do you know if you're a good leader? What input should you seek?

It's a valuable exercise to check in on how we're going with leadering in all aspects of life – work, home, family and friends.

And whilst there are many 360-degree feedback tools out there to gather data on how other people see you, they have limited use unless you've taken the time to understand what living and leading in alignment looks like for you.

If this is all sounding a bit too fluffy, understand that this will make you a better leader. It will mean you have more confidence in your skills, knowledge, and expertise, more clarity in the decisions you're making, and more motivation to do the often-challenging work of leadering.

This doesn't mean work harder.

The problem isn't that we're not working hard enough. It's that we're not working on the things that are deeply aligned with our natural inclinations and truth. Society and culture dictate 'what good looks like' and we fall into line.

So rather than focusing on what you think you want or need to *achieve*, allow some stillness to feel what it is you *yearn* for, to listen to the quiet voice of the leader you know is true to you.

What might it look like to lead and live in alignment for you?

WHAT DOES GOOD LOOK LIKE?

IGNORANCE IS ~~BLISS~~... good?

Have you ever been in a conversation with someone when you know that they don't know the answer, but are bluffing their way through? Yes. Me too. And maybe just maybe… has the person ever been you…? Yes, yes, yes! Me too.

It's a big deal to admit that you don't know the answer. The fear of humiliation or being wrong is very real.

There are powerful neurological and psychological lures in wanting and needing to have answers - a 'need for cognitive closure'. It doesn't have to be the right answer or the optimal one, as long as there are no loose ends!

The challenge for us as leaders lies with the expectations of expertise that come with our role, which make it really hard to say, 'I don't know'.

However, if we can accept there is a limit to how much we can feasibly know, we can break out of fear and insecurity and instead embrace non-knowing. With this "Don't know mind" we see everything as though for the first time. We can think with openness, let go of any preconceptions, and see things as though for the first time.

Being freed from limiting biases and beliefs, we can liberate the true nature of our intelligence and see reality – and the possibilities it holds – as it is.

How could this understanding of the not-knowing mind be an opportunity for learning, letting go and seeing things anew?

WHAT DOES GOOD LOOK LIKE?

good
STORIES

One of my favourite ways to help senior leadership teams break down silos and lead more effectively together is to invite them each to share a time when they felt proud of a contribution they made or progress they achieved.

We approach it like an artist painting a masterpiece... or an author writing a story. Starting out with an outline of the experience, gradually adding details about the journey to add colour, and finishing it off with the sparkle and texture of the people involved.

This story building and sharing is a powerful process.

It fosters reflection capacity and self-awareness through the layering process of constructing the masterpiece.

It invites confidence and clarity of what's possible going forward grounded in the lived experience of what's been done before.

And it creates deep connection and understanding that, in my experience, supersedes silos and petty politics.

Why? Because our brain processes information received through stories differently. Stories trigger the release of neurochemicals that sharpen our focus and connect us on an emotional level. They can elicit empathy and motivate us to help others.

As leaders we are often encouraged to tell stories to our people. However, asking our people to share their stories of contribution and progress could create greater confidence, clarity, connection and understanding.

Where could you encourage people to share their stories of contribution and progress?

WHAT DOES GOOD LOOK LIKE?

HOPING FOR
good

Hope.

It lifts the human spirit and helps us persevere in the face of challenge. Hope sees the positive future we can achieve if we keep moving forward, adjusting and adapting. It buoys our energy, makes life seem worthwhile, and changes our day-to-day behaviour.

Hope brings together our head, our heart and our hands, as our rational and emotional selves combine to guide our actions.

Unfortunately, in a world that is increasingly challenging and complex, hope is often seen as soft, unrealistic, and pointless. But in the world of science, hope is far more tangible.

Professor Rick Snyder, the originator of Hope Theory, defines hope as 'the process of thinking about one's goals, along with the motivation to move toward those goals (*will-power*), and the ways to achieve those goals (*way-power*).'

New research takes this beyond *will-power* and *way-power*, indicating that hope emerges from a system that also includes *who-power*, our relationships that inspire and support us, and *why-power*, the meaning and purpose behind our goals and actions.

Importantly for us as leaders, people with high hope are interested not only in their own goals, but also in the goals of others.

Hope has an emergent quality that is always available to us – if we choose to access it. When we do, we benefit from all the goodness hope brings.

Take a moment to ponder what you are hoping for... the goals that you 'want to' achieve and the *will-power, way-power, who-power* and *why-power* that could support and enable you to get there.

WHAT DOES GOOD LOOK LIKE?

"My actions are my only true belongings.
I cannot escape the consequences of my actions.
My actions are the ground on which I stand."

Thich Nhat Hanh

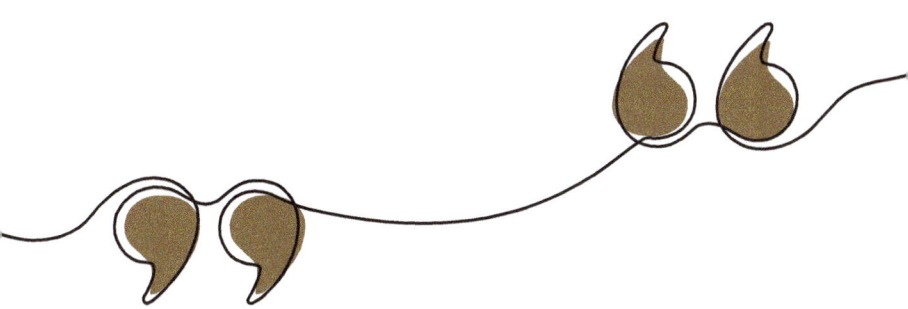

ABOUT THE AUTHOR

Dr Paige Williams is an author, researcher and PhD in Organisational Behaviour. A trusted advisor and mentor to senior leaders across business, government, education and beyond, she uses a potent blend of neuroscience, psychology and her own twenty-plus years of international business leadership experience to surface uncomfortable truths and help leaders see the rules they need to break in order to breakthrough and lead themselves, their teams, and their organisations to thrive.

The results are dramatic and measurable.

www.ingramcontent.com/pod-product-compliance
Lightning Source LLC
Chambersburg PA
CBHW062052290426
44109CB00027B/2809